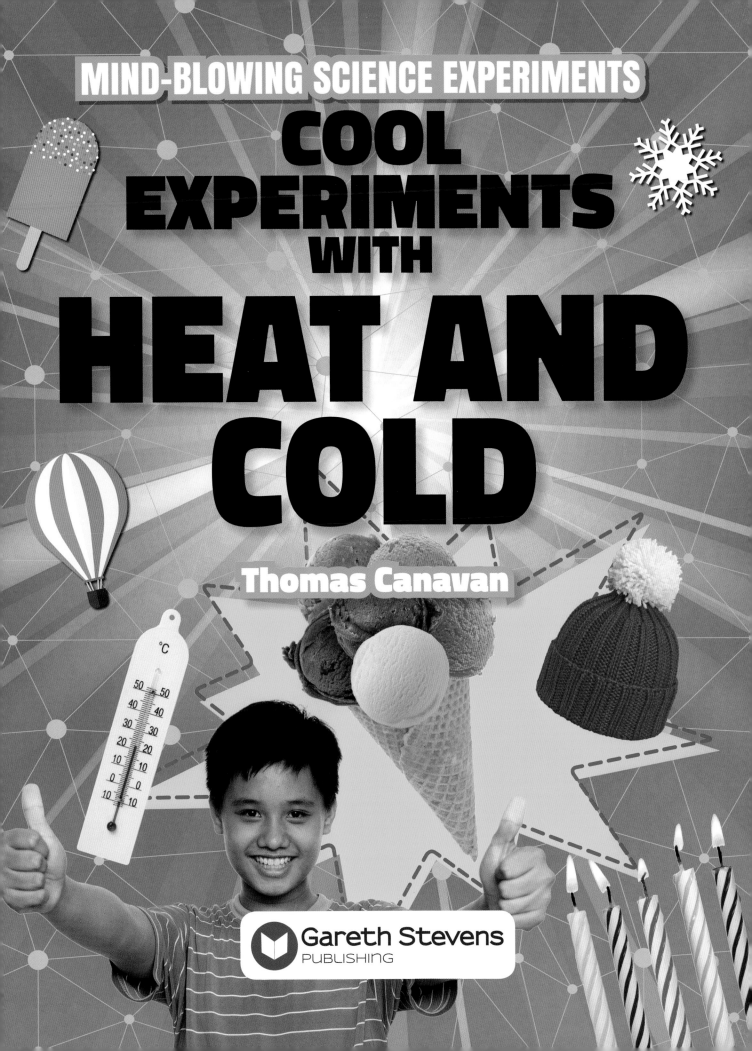

MIND-BLOWING SCIENCE EXPERIMENTS

COOL EXPERIMENTS WITH HEAT AND COLD

Thomas Canavan

Gareth Stevens
PUBLISHING

Please visit our website, www.garethstevens.com.
For a free color catalog of all our high-quality books,
call toll free 1-800-542-2595 or fax 1-877-542-2596.

Cataloging-in-Publication Data
Names: Canavan, Thomas.
Title: Cool experiments with heat and cold / Thomas Canavan.
Description: New York : Gareth Stevens Publishing, 2018. | Series: Mind-blowing science experiments | Includes index.
Identifiers: ISBN 9781538207512 (pbk.) | ISBN 9781538207413 (library bound) | ISBN 9781538207291 (6 pack)
Subjects: LCSH: Heat--Experiments--Juvenile literature. | Temperature measurements--Juvenile literature. |
    Science--Experiments--Juvenile literature.
Classification: LCC QC320.14 C317 2018 | DDC 536.078--dc23

Published in 2018 by
Gareth Stevens Publishing
111 East 14th Street, Suite 349
New York, NY 10003

Copyright © Arcturus Holdings Limited

Author: Thomas Canavan
Illustrator: Adam Linley
Experiments Coordinator: Anna Middleton
Designer: Elaine Wilkinson
Designer series edition: Emma Randall
Editors: Joe Harris, Rebecca Clunes, Frances Evans

All images courtesy of Shutterstock.

Printed in China
CPSIA compliance information: Batch CS17GS: For further information contact
Gareth Stevens, New York, New York at 1-800-542-2595.

Having Fun and Being Safe

Inside this book you'll find a whole range of exciting science experiments that can be performed safely at home. Nearly all the equipment you need will be found around your own house. Anything that you don't have at home should be available at a local store.

We have given some recommendations alongside the instructions to let you know when adult help might be needed. However, the degree of adult supervision will vary, depending on the age of the reader and the experiment. We would recommend close adult supervision for any experiment involving cooking equipment, sharp implements, electrical equipment, or batteries.

The author and publisher cannot take responsibility for any injury, damage, or mess that might occur as a result of attempting the experiments in this book. Always tell an adult before you perform any experiments, and follow the instructions carefully.

Contents

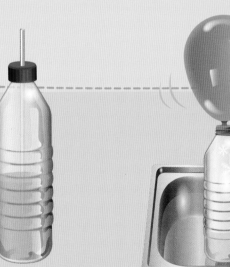

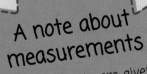

A note about measurements

Measurements are given in U.S. form with metric in parentheses. The metric conversion is rounded to make it easier to measure.

Who knew science could be so cool? Or hot! Get ready to explore the extremes of heat and cold with these mind-blowing experiments!

Water Race

Does your face ever look flushed and red when you've been running? There's a scientific reason for that—and you can demonstrate it with just a few odds and ends from your own kitchen.

YOU WILL NEED

- 4 glasses that can hold 5 fluid ounces (150 ml) each
- 2 paper towels
- Hot water
- Cold water

1

Roll each paper towel into a long, tight tube.

2

Fill one glass with cold water and another with hot water.

3
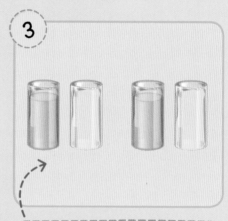
Place an empty glass next to each of the filled glasses.

4
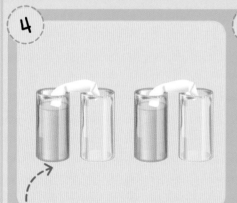
Place one end of each paper tube in the filled glasses. Place the dry ends of the paper tubes in the empty glasses.

5
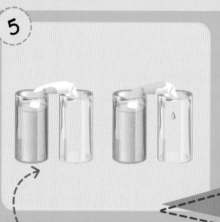
Observe which glass delivers water to its empty partner first.

You don't need to use scalding water for this experiment. Get the water as hot as you can while staying within your comfort zone.

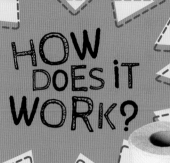

HOW DOES IT WORK?

This experiment demonstrates osmosis, a process that sends water from a denser solution into a less dense solution. Water is denser than air, so the water in your filled glasses traveled to the empty glasses. Within the paper towels, there are tiny air tubes called **capillaries**. The water travels through these capillaries to the empty glasses. This is called capillary motion. Heat increases the **kinetic energy** of **molecules**, so the warm-water molecules travel faster than their colder rivals. In both cases, though, the water is pushed upwards by capillary action and then drawn down into the empty cup through **gravity**.

TOP TIP!

It doesn't really matter what type of glass you use, but clear plastic or glass gives you the best chance to observe the first drips.

WHAT HAPPENS IF...?

What would happen after a few hours? If you wait, you'll have the chance to observe another aspect of science — **equilibrium**. Eventually, the warm water will cool and the capillary motion/gravity seesaw will stop. All four cups will hold the same level of water!

REAL-LIFE SCIENCE

Your smallest blood vessels are capillaries. When you get warmer — like after a run — more blood rushes through the capillaries just beneath your skin to help your body cool down. This causes your face to "flush" red. It's the same basic process at work with your cups, towels, and water!

Heating Up

What do a tower of soup cans and circling birds of prey have in common? You'll find out in this experiment! The answer is all about **convection**, the term used to describe what happens when air warms up—or cools down!

YOU WILL NEED

- 3 empty soup cans
- Can opener
- Sticky tack
- Masking tape
- 2 paper clips
- Thumbtack
- Ruler
- Pencil
- Printer paper
- 2 large books of equal size
- Table near a sunny window

1

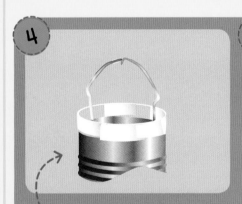

Ask an adult to open the cans and throw away the lids. Then ask them to help you tape the rim of each can with masking tape.

2

Stack the cans to make a tower. Secure each can to the next with masking tape.

3

Straighten out the paper clips. Tape them both to the inside of top can's rim, pointing up. They should be opposite each other and sticking down about ½ inch (1 cm) inside the can.

4

Carefully bend the free ends of the clips so that they meet and form an arch.

5

Strengthen this arch with a little tape where the clips meet, then place a small, pea-sized ball of sticky tack on top.

6

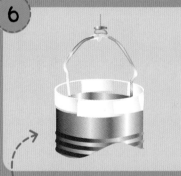

Carefully press the thumbtack (pointing up) onto the sticky tack.

6

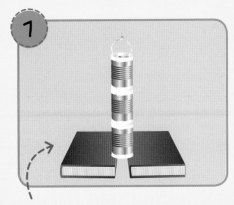

7

Lay the books on the table about 2 inches (5 cm) apart. Set the tower over the gap between the books. It should rest equally on each book.

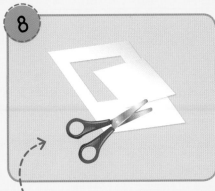

8

Cut the paper into a 6 × 6 -inch (15 × 15 cm) square.

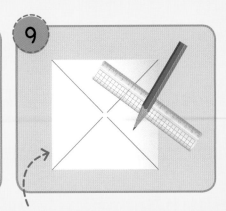

9

Use the ruler to mark a line from each corner of the paper towards the center. Step each line about ¼ inch (5 mm) from the center.

10

Cut along the lines you've just drawn.

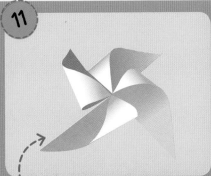

11

Bend every other corner of the paper down to the center and tape them all in place. You should have a pinwheel shape.

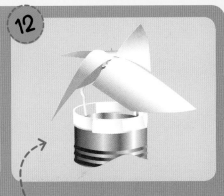

12

Carefully balance the pinwheel (taped side down) on the point of the drawing pin.

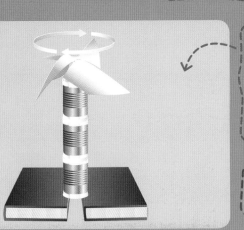

13

When exposed to sunlight, the pinwheel should start to spin.

Continued

Be careful when using the scissors and thumbtack.

HOW DOES IT WORK?

Warm air rises because its molecules move around more freely. The air becomes less dense—and lighter. The sun shining on your tower heats up the air inside it, and the warm air rises up through the tower. Leaving the gap at the bottom of the tower allows more air to rush in, filling the space of the warm air that flowed up. The rising air spins your handmade pinwheel at the top! This **vertical** movement of air is called convection. Cooling temperatures can cause air and other substances to sink—this is also convection.

TOP TIP!

Although you want the arms of the pinwheel to be secure, it's a good idea to trim the excess tape at the joints. This keeps the pinwheel's arms lighter.

WHAT HAPPENS IF...?

Although this experiment works best on a sunny day with a window able to capture the heat, you could make some interesting observations on a day with changeable weather. Or you could observe the motion of the pinwheel each day for a week. Did you notice any difference in the speed of the pinwheel? Why is that?

REAL-LIFE SCIENCE

Convection plays an important part in how our weather develops and changes. You've probably seen those puffy cumulus clouds towering high into the sky. Convection fluffs them up like that! Hang-gliders and soaring birds such as buzzards can capture updrafts to stay aloft, sometimes for hours.

Handmade Thermometer

YOU WILL NEED

- Empty plastic bottle
- Plastic straw
- Sticky tack
- Water
- Food coloring
- Sharp knife and an adult to help you

Old-fashioned bulb thermometers have a column of mercury inside a glass tube. As things get warmer, the mercury expands and rises up the column. Markings alongside it equate to degrees. You can use a similar principle with good old air and water to make your own thermometer!

1

Fill the bottle halfway with cold water.

2

Add a few drops of food coloring and swirl the bottle so that the water is evenly colored.

An adult should use the knife to cut the hole in the bottle cap.

3

Ask an adult to cut a hole in the bottle cap. It should be just big enough for the straw to pass through.

4

Screw the lid onto the bottle.

5

Slide the straw through the hole so that the bottom is below water level but not touching the bottom of the bottle.

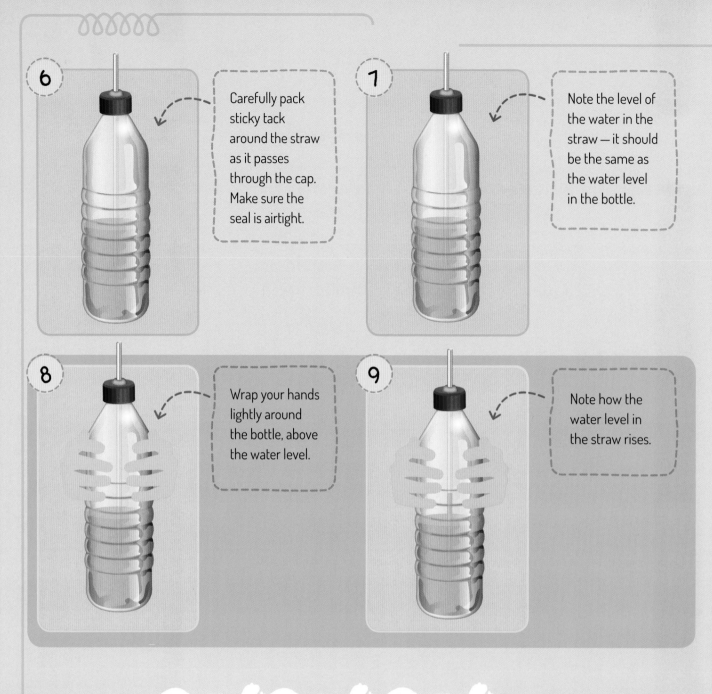

6 Carefully pack sticky tack around the straw as it passes through the cap. Make sure the seal is airtight.

7 Note the level of the water in the straw — it should be the same as the water level in the bottle.

8 Wrap your hands lightly around the bottle, above the water level.

9 Note how the water level in the straw rises.

TOP TiPS!

You can get a quicker, more dramatic result if you rub your hands together briskly for a few seconds before gripping the bottle. The friction will make your hands much warmer, which will heat up the bottle faster!

You get the best results with a clear straw, but water that's darkened with extra food coloring will show through most straws.

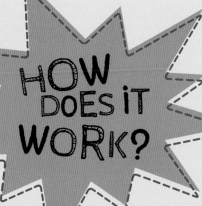

HOW DOES IT WORK?

As any substance gets warmer, its molecules become more active. That extra activity means that **gases** begin to take up more **volume**. That's what happened here. Your hand warmed the air (gas) inside the bottle. The air expanded and began to push on the water because it needed more space. That pressure, in turn, pushed water up the straw. The warmer the air became, the more it expanded, and the higher the water rose in the straw!

REAL-LIFE SCIENCE

Don't forget, you haven't created more air in this experiment. You've simply allowed it to expand. If the same amount of a gas (such as air) fills more space, it becomes less dense. That means it is lighter, which is why the less-dense air in hot-air balloons provides all that lift!

WHAT HAPPENS IF...?

What would happen if you purposefully disobeyed steps 5 and 6 of this experiment? If the straw doesn't extend below the water, the expanding warmer air simply escapes through the straw. The air will also find a way out if the seal on the cap has gaps. In other words, your thermometer won't work!

Candle Seesaw

It's easy to have fun with forces—just look at seesaws! This experiment turns up the heat with a fire-powered seesaw! You'll have to see it to believe it! Grab an adult to help you and prepare to be amazed.

YOU WILL NEED

- Candle, about 6 inches (15 cm) long and 1 inch (2 cm) wide
- Long, narrow nail
- 2 identical drinking glasses
- 2 saucers
- Table
- Sharp knife
- Matches
- An adult to help you

1

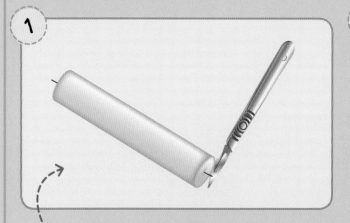

Ask an adult to scrape away some of the wax at the flat end of the candle to expose the wick.

2

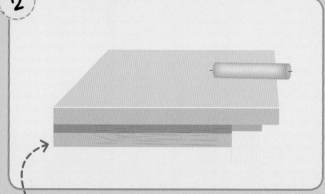

Lay the candle on the table so that one end hangs slightly over the edge.

3

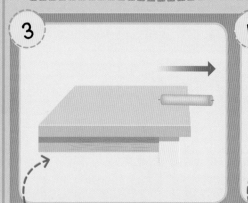

Push the candle gently towards the edge. When it begins to tip, catch it and hold it in place.

4

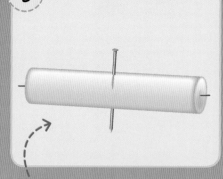

Ask an adult to mark the balancing point with the tip of the knife.

5

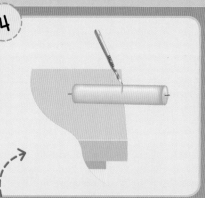

Ask an adult to slide the nail through the candle's balancing point. The same length of nail should stick out on both sides of the candle.

6

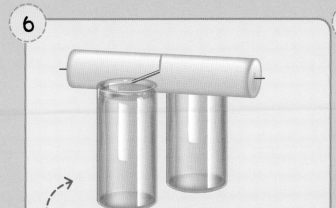

Line the glasses up side-by-side and balance the candle by resting the jutting nail on the glass rims. To avoid wax dripping on the table, you can place a saucer under each end of the candle.

7

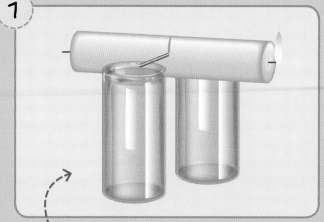

Have an adult light one end of the candle and then wait a few seconds until the lit end rises up.

8

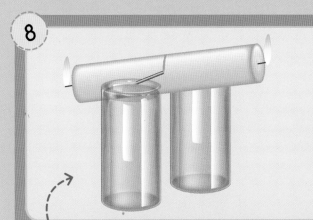

Now ask the adult to light the other end of the candle.

9

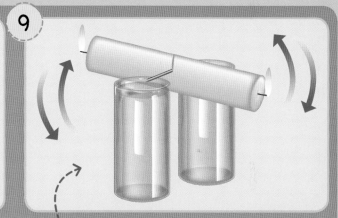

Soon the candle will be moving up and down like a seesaw!

It's always important to have an adult light matches and candles.

TOP TIP!

Try to find a nail that is long and narrow so that it goes through the candle without breaking it.

Continued ➡

HOW DOES IT WORK?

Although this is a simple demonstration on one level, a lot is going on. Heat—an energy by-product of combustion—is the driving force of this experiment. Oxygen from the air provides much of the "fuel" for the chemical reaction, and thermal energy (heat) is released. That heat melts the wax. When some of the melted wax drips off, that end of the candle loses mass and goes up, like a seesaw. Then the lower side burns more, loses more mass, and swings up! The cycle continues.

WHAT HAPPENS IF...?

If you have a good supply of candles and an adult to help you, then you could try using candles of different lengths for this experiment. You can change the speed of a normal seesaw by moving closer to or further away from the person on the other end. Do you think the candle length would affect this experiment? Test it and see for yourself!

REAL-LIFE SCIENCE

Heat and flames produce a rhythm in something that you know very well—cars. An electrical spark causes gas fumes to **ignite** and expand in cylinders inside the engine. The expanding gas pushes pistons up, and cooling gas lets them come down again. This up-and-down motion is fast and constant, and it provides the "drive" that moves the car.

the Pizza Oven

Were your eyes bigger than your stomach when you ordered pizza last night? Here's a chance to harness solar power to reheat those leftovers! Just make sure you do this experiment on a sunny day.

YOU WILL NEED

- A cardboard pizza box
- Ruler
- Kitchen foil
- Black construction paper
- Saran wrap
- Glue stick
- Packing tape
- Scissors
- Felt-tip pen
- Slice of pizza

1

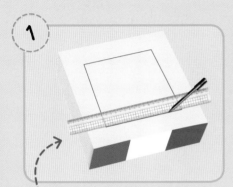

Use a ruler and felt-tip pen to draw a square shape on the top flap of the pizza box. Draw it about 1 inch (2 cm) in from the four edges.

2

Cut along three of those four lines, leaving the line along the hinge of the box alone. Open and close several times to form a crease.

> Take care with the scissors when you cut the pizza box.

3

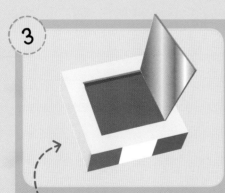

Cut a piece of foil the same size as this flap. Glue it to the inside edge of the flap. This will reflect sunlight down into the box.

4

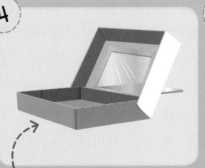

Cut a piece of Saran wrap just a bit larger than the opening. Use the packing tape to attach it to the underside of the box top. Make sure it covers the cut-out hole completely.

5

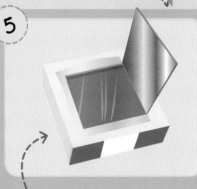

Repeat step 4, attaching the second piece of Saran wrap to the other side of the cut-out hole.

15

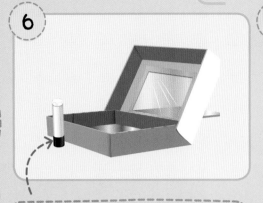

Cut a second piece of foil and glue it to the bottom (inside) of the pizza box. This piece will act as **insulation**.

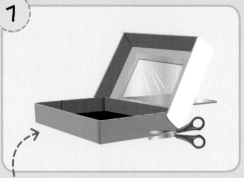

Cut black construction paper to fit the inside of this same base. Tape it to the foil on the base. It will help absorb heat.

By now, the box top should have a seal made of Saran wrap covering the hole. The foil-backed flap should open up from seal.

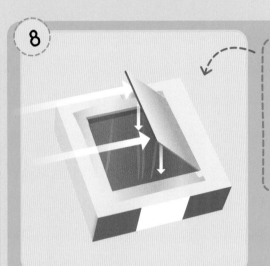

Aim the box so that it opens towards the Sun. Prop the flap open but keep the box top shut.

Place a piece of pizza in the oven.

Leave the pizza in the oven until it is hot enough to eat. You can heat up all sorts of things in your oven! Why not try marshmallows next?

Although this oven doesn't get as hot as the one in your kitchen, leave the flap open a few seconds before putting your hand in. This gives it time to cool a little.

HOW DOES IT WORK?

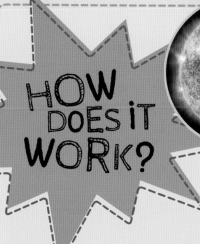

You've tied together lots of different scientific ideas with this one experiment. The main ingredient, of course, is the solar power—the heat from sunlight. Some of it would pass straight through the clear plastic anyway, but the extra foil on the open flap focuses even more energy towards the base. The plastic allows energy to pass into the box and prevents it from escaping. And black—the color of the paper on the base—absorbs more heat energy than other colors. The lower layer of foil adds even more insulating help!

TOP TIP!

If you have sheets of PVC and an adult to cut them for you, you could use PVC instead of Saran wrap.

WHAT HAPPENS IF...?

You can easily see how this demonstration of solar power works by deliberately not following some of these instructions. With no foil on the flap above, the oven will have less fuel and the food won't heat as much. Try the experiment with just one element missing—for example, the foil on the flap—and see how it works out.

REAL-LIFE SCIENCE

You've probably seen curved satellite dishes. Like your oven, they're designed to reflect radiation and direct it to a single point. Your "single point" is the base of the oven. A satellite dish has a receiver to pick up signals that have bounced off the curve. It sends these signals along cables to your TV!

Ice Cream Chiller

YOU WILL NEED

- 2 bowls
- Ice cream
- Ice cream scooper
- 2 spoons
- Milk
- A friend

After all this disciplined scientific experimenting, don't you deserve a treat? How about a delicious bowl of ice cream—or better yet, two? Science and ice cream? Talk about a win-win situation!

1

Put two scoops of ice cream in each bowl.

2

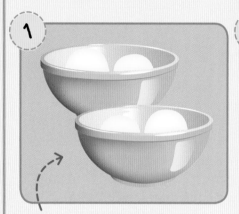

Ask a friend to taste some of the ice cream in the first bowl, paying particular attention to how cold it feels.

3

Pour spoonfuls of milk into the second bowl until you've completely covered the ice cream.

4

Now ask your friend to repeat step 2 with the second bowl of ice cream.

5

Ask your friend to alternate between bowls, having a spoonful from one, then a spoonful from the other. You might need to take part in this experiment as well, if you haven't begun to do so already. Do you agree that the milk-coated ice cream tastes—or feels—colder?

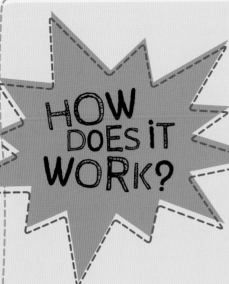

HOW DOES IT WORK?

Things feel colder when they help transfer heat away from you. That's why metals feel colder than wood. We know that ice cream is cold, but it is also full of tiny bubbles. They're what give it that soft texture. But air is also a great insulator, which means that it slows the transfer of heat from one thing to another. Milk doesn't have all those bubbles. This means that the heat from your tongue or lips passes more easily through the milk (making it feel colder) than it does through the ice cream (with all those insulating bubbles).

TOP TIP!

You can vary this experiment by using different flavors. You could also compare ice cream that has just come out of the freezer to slightly melted ice cream.

WHAT HAPPENS IF...?

This experiment depends on the difference in consistency between the ice cream and the milk. What do you suppose would happen if you put some regular ice cream and some milk-covered ice cream back in the freezer? Try it! Use paper cups rather than bowls that might crack. Make a **prediction** and see what happens.

REAL-LIFE SCIENCE

Farming villages in parts of Russia once held big celebrations when winter's first snow fell. That might seem strange, considering that their fields would be covered in snow for the next six months. They celebrated because the snow protected the crops underneath. Fallen snow is actually full of air, which means that the snow is really more of a blanket to keep the much colder air out. Under the snow it isn't exactly warm, but it remains a lot warmer than the bitter air outside.

Greenhouse Effect

Earth's climate is changing—and that is a cause for alarm. Our planet has warmed and cooled quite naturally over millions of years, but recent surface temperature rises are most likely due to human activity. Why? Here's an experiment to help you understand.

1 Fill both glasses almost to the brim with cold water from the tap.

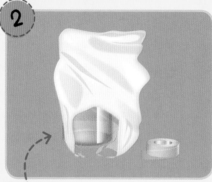

2 Carefully slide the bag around one glass, and seal it shut.

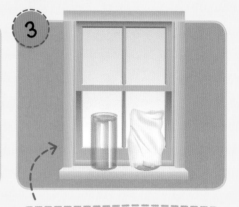

3 Place both glasses on a sunny windowsill. If it's cloudy, place them about 20 inches (50 cm) below a reading lamp.

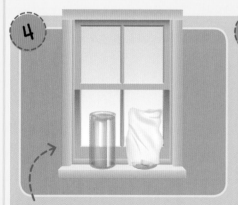

4 Leave the glasses for two hours.

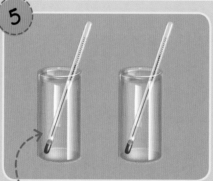

5 Undo the plastic bag and take the temperature of the water in both glasses.

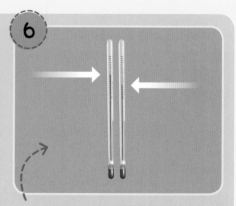

6 Note which water is warmer.

HOW DOES IT WORK?

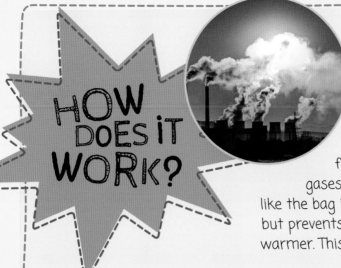

You've just demonstrated the effects of climate change—on a very small scale. Think of the water in the glasses as the Earth's oceans, and the air around the glasses as the Earth's atmosphere. Heat energy reaches the oceans from the Sun. Smoke from factories, exhaust from cars and other gases can form a "blanket" around the Earth, just like the bag in this experiment. The blanket lets heat in, but prevents some of it from escaping, so the water gets warmer. This process is called the "greenhouse effect."

TOP TIP!

Make sure the glasses are identical, so the results are more accurate. Glasses made of glass work best.

WHAT HAPPENS IF...?

If you have a period of changeable weather ahead of you, why not try the same experiment each day for a week? Does the "sandwich bag" water heat up even on cloudy days? How about trying the experiment with three different-sized glasses, each inside a bag. Do they warm up to the same degree?

REAL-LIFE SCIENCE

The effects of climate change are often measured in ocean temperatures. An overall rise of just one degree Celsius might not sound like much, but it would cause a lot of damage. Some of the planet's ice caps would begin to melt, raising sea levels and threatening low-lying areas around the world.

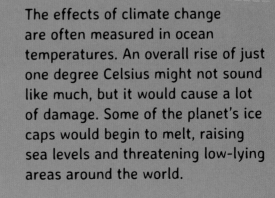

Hot-air Balloon

This experiment will take you back over 200 years to the dawn of a groundbreaking technology—the hot-air balloon. This invention ultimately led to planes and helicopters. Prepare to launch this aircraft from your own house!

YOU WILL NEED

- 2 sheets each of red and blue tissue paper, 20 × 30 inches (50 × 75 cm) each
- Water-based glue
- Scissors
- Felt-tip pen
- Piece of card stock
- Hair dryer

1

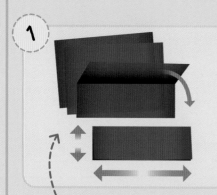

Fold each sheet in half along the short side. Each should measure 10 × 30 inches (25 × 75 cm). Lay each sheet down with the folded edge facing towards you.

2

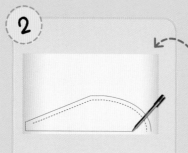

Copy the template design (shown here) onto the piece of card stock. The upright side on the left should be 2 inches (5 cm) tall and the other straight edge should be 24 inches (60 cm) long.

3

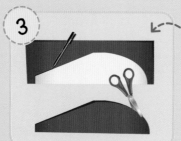

Cut out the template and trace its shape along each of the four pieces of tissue paper. The 24-inch (60 cm) straight edge should run along the fold of the tissue paper.

4

Carefully cut each of the pieces of tissue paper and unfold them. Glue the four pieces together, overlapping the pieces as shown here. Make sure that the mouth of the balloon, where the 2-inch (5 cm) sections join, can still open.

5

Hold the balloon just above the hair dryer. Turn the dryer on to the "warm" setting. Watch the balloon fill with air, then release it.

HOW DOES IT WORK?

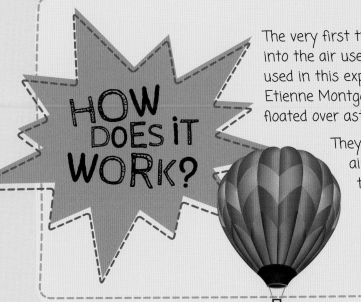

The very first type of man-made object to carry passengers into the air used some of the same methods that you've just used in this experiment. In 1783, Joseph-Ralf and Jacques-Etienne Montgolfier took off in the first hot-air balloon and floated over astounded observers in France.

They used a simple principle. By warming the air inside the balloon, they made it less dense than the surrounding air. That meant that it would "float" on the outside air as long as the air inside was warm. You've done exactly the same thing with your balloon and hair dryer!

WHAT HAPPENS IF...?

You can see the difference that heat makes if you fill the balloon with air when the hair dryer is set to "cool." Any idea about what might—or might not—happen?

REAL-LIFE SCIENCE

Hot-air balloons are still a popular way of enjoying sights from above, but you'd need huge balloons and furnaces to lift more than a few people. That's why modern airships use gases such as helium inside their "balloon" parts. Like heated air, they are less dense than the air around them—"lighter than air," in fact.

TOP TIPS!

Ask an adult to hold the balloon above the hair dryer as you fill the balloon.

Take care not to let the balloon get too close to the hair dryer.

A Lot of Hot Air?

Do you ever get tired or feel out of breath from blowing up balloons? Wouldn't it be great if balloons could just inflate themselves? Well, you can use science to do some of the job! It might not be quick, but it's a good way to save your breath.

1

Feed the balloon over the top of the empty bottle. Make sure it covers all the twists in the mouth of the bottle and is firmly in place.

Put the bottle (with the attached balloon) into the freezer for 30 minutes.

2

3

Just before the 30-minute mark, fill 2/3 of the sink with hot water.

4

Take the bottle from the freezer and stand it in the hot water, making sure the water does not get into the bottle.

5

Watch the balloon begin to inflate by itself!

24

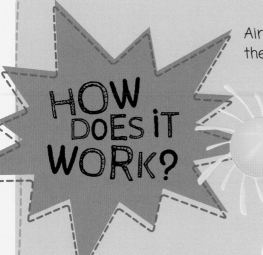

HOW DOES IT WORK?

Air is a gas made up of many, many molecules (which themselves are combinations of **atoms**). Those molecules move around more, and take up more space, when they are warm. They move around less, and take up less space, as they cool.

The air inside the bottle and balloon "shrank" when it was in the freezer, but expanded again when it came out. As the bottle warmed in the hot water, the air inside it expanded enough to fill the balloon.

TOP TIPS!

Hot tap water can be VERY hot sometimes. Be careful!

WHAT HAPPENS IF...?

Not convinced? Take several balloons and repeat the experiment a number of times at different temperatures. Try it outside on a cold day or in the fridge. Record your results. You can also try attaching a balloon to a bottle and simply leaving it where it is, on the table at room temperature, for 30 minutes. What do you think will happen?

REAL-LIFE SCIENCE

Many liquids take up more space when they have been warmed up to produce a gas. A steam engine works by heating water until it becomes a gas – water vapor. The water vapor expands and pushes mechanical parts back and forth, or around and around. It can even power something as big and heavy as a train!

The Fickle Flame

YOU WILL NEED

- Large table or other sturdy, flat surface
- Sticky tack
- Tea light
- Matches and an adult to help you
- Glass mixing bowl
- Tray (large enough to hold the mixing bowl upside down)

Sometimes you get a chance to show off lots of your scientific knowledge with just one experiment! This demonstration lets you show how one principle can affect another.

1

Roll a ball of sticky tack and set it in the middle of the tray to act as a base for the tea light.

2

Set the tea light on the base and place the mixing bowl over it like a dome.

Make sure an adult lights the matches and candle.

3

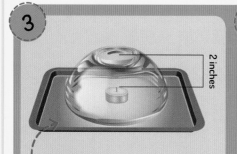

2 inches

Slide the tray back and forth slightly to make sure the tea light is secure. Strengthen the base if it isn't.

4

Remove the bowl and place four pea-sized balls of sticky tack along the rim, evenly spaced. They will act as soft bases when the bowl is overturned later.

5

Make sure there is at least 2 inches (5 cm) of space between the top of the tea light and the top of the bowl.

6 Ask an adult to light the tea light. Let the flame settle for a few seconds.

7 Slide the tray gently to the right and notice how the flame points to the left.

8 Return the tray to its original position. If the tea light went out, ask an adult to re-light it.

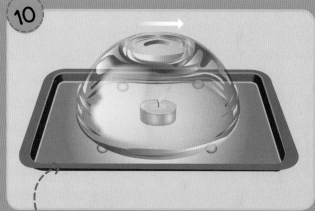

9 With an adult's help, carefully lower the upside-down bowl over the lit tea light. Make sure the flame is steady.

10 Repeat step 7. This time, the flame moves to the right!

You don't want the glass to become too hot, so blow out the candle after about 10 seconds.

TOP TIP!

You might need some practice in moving the tray quickly enough to get a reaction from the flame — but not so fast that the fire gets snuffed out.

HOW DOES IT WORK?

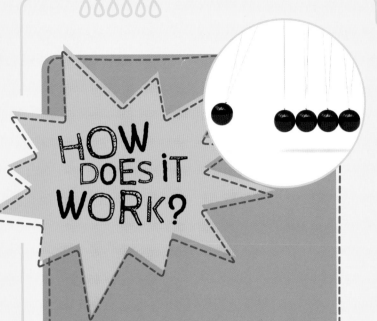

You called on several different scientific principles in this simple experiment. Newton's First Law of Motion says that an object will stay at rest—or continue moving—unless an outside force acts on it. Moving the candle counts as an outside force, so the flame lags behind—when it's not covered. When it is covered, the flame heats the air near it and makes it less dense. The air inside the container further away from the tea light lags behind, just like the flame in step 7. You can't see it, but the cooler air is bunched at the back of the moving container, pushing the hotter air and the flame forwards.

You have experienced two scientific principles at work here. When you're in a car and the light turns green, you feel pushed back as the car starts to move forward. That's called **inertia**, and it's the same principle that "drags" the flame in step 7.

Heaters cause the air of a hot-air balloon to expand and become less dense. This is what happened to the air heated by the flame under the bowl!

WHAT HAPPENS IF...?

Imagine if the "base" of the upturned bowl were much higher than the four pea-sized blobs of sticky tack. If the tea light burned long enough, warm air would eventually fill the bowl, pushing the heavier, cooler air out through the bigger gap below. What would happen to the flame if you moved the tray then?

Glossary

air pressure The constant pressing of air on everything it touches.

atom The smallest particle that can exist.

capillary A very thin tube.

convection Movement of a fluid substance caused by heat.

density The amount of mass something has in relation to its volume (or space that it takes up).

equilibrium When opposite forces are balanced.

gas A substance that can expand to fill any shape.

gravity The force that causes all objects to be attracted to each other.

ignite To catch fire or begin to burn.

inertia Staying unchanged until changed by an external force.

insulation Material that prevents or slows the transfer of energy from one object to another.

kinetic energy The energy of movement.

molecule The smallest unit of a substance, such as oxygen, that has all the properties of that substance.

prediction A guess about what will happen in the future as a result of an action.

vertical Standing upright, being at right angles with the horizontal.

volume The amount of space a substance takes up inside a container.

Further Information

Books to read

Science FAQs: Why Do Ice Cubes Float? by Thomas Canavan (Franklin Watts, 2016)

Science Secrets: Secrets of Heat and Cold by Carol Ballard (Franklin Watts, 2014)

Whizzy Science: Make it Change by Anna Claybourne (Wayland, 2014)

Websites

https://www.education.com/activity/heat+and+cold/
Find incredible experiments with heat and cold at this awesome website.

http://www.dkfindout.com/us/science/heat/
Learn more about heat at this sizzling site!

http://inspirationlaboratories.com/20-temperature-experiments-and-activities/
Check out this site for cool — and hot — experiments!

Publisher's note to educators and parents: Our editors have carefully reviewed these websites to ensure that they are suitable for students. Many websites change frequently, however, and we cannot guarantee that a site's future contents will continue to meet our high standards of quality and educational value. Be advised that students should be closely supervised whenever they access the Internet.

Index